www.osha.gov

Guidelines for Preventing Workplace Violence for Health Care & Social Service Workers

U.S. Department of Labor

Occupational Safety and Health Administration

OSHA 3148-01R
2004

Contents

Notice...3

Acknowledgments...4

Introduction...4

Overview of Guidelines...7

Violence Prevention Programs...8

    Management Commitment and Employee Involvement...10

    Worksite Analysis...11

    Hazard Prevention and Control...14

    Safety and Health Training...19

    Recordkeeping and Program Evaluation...21

Conclusion...24

References...25

OSHA assistance...25

    Safety and Health Program Management Guidelines...25

    State Programs...26

    Consultation Services...26

    Voluntary Protection Programs (VPP)...27

    Strategic Partnership Program...27

    Alliance Programs...28

    OSHA Training and Education...28

    Information Available Electronically...29

    OSHA Publications...29

    Contacting OSHA...30

OSHA Regional Offices...30

Appendices

Appendix A: Workplace Violence Program Checklists...32

Appendix B: Violence Incident Report Forms...40

Appendix C: Suggested Readings...42

Notice

These guidelines are not a new standard or regulation. They are advisory in nature, informational in content and intended to help employers establish effective workplace violence prevention programs adapted to their specific worksites. The guidelines do not address issues related to patient care. They are performance-oriented, and how employers implement them will vary based on the site's hazard analysis.

Violence inflicted on employees may come from many sources— external parties such as robbers or muggers and internal parties such as coworkers and patients. These guidelines address only the violence inflicted by patients or clients against staff. However, OSHA suggests that workplace violence policies indicate a zero-tolerance for all forms of violence from all sources.

The *Occupational Safety and Health Act of 1970 (OSH Act)*[1] mandates that, in addition to compliance with hazard-specific standards, all employers have a general duty to provide their employees with a workplace free from recognized hazards likely to cause death or serious physical harm. OSHA will rely on Section 5(a)(1) of the *OSH Act*, the "General Duty Clause,"[2] for enforcement authority. Failure to implement these guidelines is not in itself a violation of the General Duty Clause. However, employers can be cited for violating the General Duty Clause if there is a recognized hazard of workplace violence in their establishments and they do nothing to prevent or abate it.

When Congress passed the *OSH Act*, it recognized that workers' compensation systems provided state-specific remedies for job-related injuries and illnesses. Determining what constitutes a compensable claim and the rate of compensation were left to the states, their legislatures and their courts. Congress acknowledged this point in Section 4(b)(4) of the *OSH Act*, when it stated categorically: "Nothing in this chapter shall be construed to supersede or in any manner affect any workmen's compensation law. . .."[3] Therefore,

---

[1] Public Law 91-596, December 29, 1970; and as amended by P.L. 101-552, Section 3101, November 5, 1990.

[2] "Each employer shall furnish to each of his employees employment and a place of employment which are free from recognized hazards that are causing or are likely to cause death or serious physical harm to his employees."

[3] 29 U.S.C. 653(b)(4).

these non-mandatory guidelines should not be viewed as enlarging or diminishing the scope of work-related injuries. The guidelines are intended for use in any state and without regard to whether any injuries or fatalities are later determined to be compensable.

Acknowledgments

Many people have contributed to these guidelines. They include health care, social service and employee assistance experts; researchers; educators; unions and other stakeholders; OSHA professionals; and the National Institute for Occupational Safety and Health (NIOSH).

Also, several states have developed relevant standards or recommendations, such as California OSHA's *CAL/OSHA Guidelines for Workplace Security and Guidelines for Security and Safety of Health Care and Community Service Workers*; New Jersey Public Employees Occupational Safety and Health's *Guidelines on Measures and Safeguards in Dealing with Violent or Aggressive Behavior in Public Sector Health Care Facilities*; and the State of Washington Department of Labor and Industries' *Violence in Washington Workplaces and Study of Assaults on Staff in Washington State Psychiatric Hospitals*. Other organizations with relevant recommendations include the Joint Commission on Accreditation of Health Care Organizations' *Comprehensive Accreditation Manuals for Hospitals*, the Metropolitan Chicago Healthcare Council's *Guidelines for Dealing with Violence in Health Care*, and the American Nurses Association's *Promoting Safe Work Environments for Nurses*. These and other agencies have information available to assist employers.

Introduction

Workplace violence affects health care and social service workers.

The National Institute for Occupational Safety and Health (NIOSH) defines workplace violence as "violent acts (including physical assaults and threats of assaults) directed toward persons at work or on duty."[4] This includes terrorism as illustrated by the

[4]CDC/NIOSH. Violence. Occupational Hazards in Hospitals. 2002.

4

terrorist acts of September 11, 2001 that resulted in the deaths of 2,886 workers in New York, Virginia and Pennsylvania. Although these guidelines do not address terrorism specifically, this type of violence remains a threat to U.S. workplaces.

For many years, health care and social service workers have faced a significant risk of job-related violence. Assaults represent a serious safety and health hazard within these industries. OSHA's violence prevention guidelines provide the agency's recommenda-tions for reducing workplace violence, developed following a careful review of workplace violence studies, public and private violence prevention programs and input from stakeholders. OSHA encourages employers to establish violence prevention programs and to track their progress in reducing work-related assaults. Although not every incident can be prevented, many can, and the severity of injuries sustained by employees can be reduced. Adopting practical measures such as those outlined here can significantly reduce this serious threat to worker safety.

Extent of the problem

The Bureau of Labor Statistics (BLS) reports that there were 69 homicides in the health services from 1996 to 2000. Although workplace homicides may attract more attention, the vast majority of workplace violence consists of non-fatal assaults. BLS data shows that in 2000, 48 percent of all non-fatal injuries from occupational assaults and violent acts occurred in health care and social services. Most of these occurred in hospitals, nursing and personal care facilities, and residential care services. Nurses, aides, orderlies and attendants suffered the most non-fatal assaults resulting in injury.

Injury rates also reveal that health care and social service workers are at high risk of violent assault at work. BLS rates measure the number of events per 10,000 full-time workers—in this case, assaults resulting in injury. In 2000, health service workers overall had an incidence rate of 9.3 for injuries resulting from assaults and violent acts. The rate for social service workers was 15, and for nursing and personal care facility workers, 25. This compares to an overall private sector injury rate of 2.

The Department of Justice's (DOJ) National Crime Victimization Survey for 1993 to 1999 lists average annual rates of non-fatal violent crime by occupation. The average annual rate for non-fatal

violent crime for all occupations is 12.6 per 1,000 workers. The average annual rate for physicians is 16.2; for nurses, 21.9; for mental health professionals, 68.2; and for mental health custodial workers, 69. (*Note:* These data do not compare directly to the BLS figures because DOJ presents violent incidents per 1,000 workers and BLS displays injuries involving days away from work per 10,000 workers. Both sources, however, reveal the same high risk for health care and social service workers.)

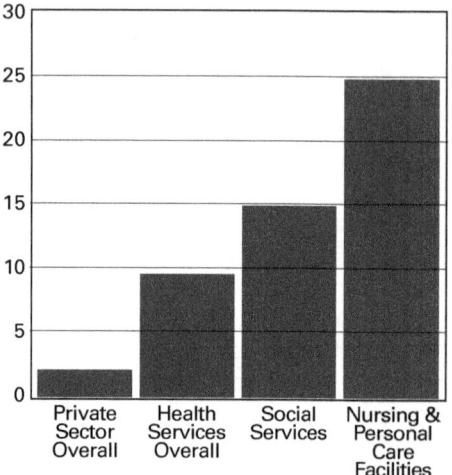

Incidence rates for nonfatal assaults and violent acts by industry, 2000

Incidence rate per 10,000 full-time workers

Source: U.S. Department of Labor, Bureau of Labor Statistics. (2001). *Survey of Occupational Injuries and Illnesses,* 2000.

As significant as these numbers are, the actual number of incidents is probably much higher. Incidents of violence are likely to be underreported, perhaps due in part to the persistent perception within the health care industry that assaults are part of the job. Underreporting may reflect a lack of institutional reporting policies, employee beliefs that reporting will not benefit them or employee fears that employers may deem assaults the result of employee negligence or poor job performance.

The risk factors

Health care and social service workers face an increased risk of work-related assaults stemming from several factors. These include:

- The prevalence of handguns and other weapons among patients, their families or friends;

- The increasing use of hospitals by police and the criminal justice system for criminal holds and the care of acutely disturbed, violent individuals;

- The increasing number of acute and chronic mentally ill patients being released from hospitals without follow-up care (these

patients have the right to refuse medicine and can no longer be hospitalized involuntarily unless they pose an immediate threat to themselves or others);

- The availability of drugs or money at hospitals, clinics and pharmacies, making them likely robbery targets;
- Factors such as the unrestricted movement of the public in clinics and hospitals and long waits in emergency or clinic areas that lead to client frustration over an inability to obtain needed services promptly;
- The increasing presence of gang members, drug or alcohol abusers, trauma patients or distraught family members;
- Low staffing levels during times of increased activity such as mealtimes, visiting times and when staff are transporting patients;
- Isolated work with clients during examinations or treatment;
- Solo work, often in remote locations with no backup or way to get assistance, such as communication devices or alarm systems (this is particularly true in high-crime settings);
- Lack of staff training in recognizing and managing escalating hostile and assaultive behavior; and
- Poorly lit parking areas.

Overview of Guidelines

In January 1989, OSHA published voluntary, generic safety and health program management guidelines for all employers to use as a foundation for their safety and health programs, which can include workplace violence prevention programs.[5] OSHA's violence prevention guidelines build on these generic guidelines by identifying common risk factors and describing some feasible solutions. Although not exhaustive, the workplace violence guidelines include policy recommendations and practical corrective methods to help prevent and mitigate the effects of workplace violence.

[5]OSHA's Safety and Health Program Management Guidelines (54 *Federal Register* (16):3904–3916, January 26, 1989).

The goal is to eliminate or reduce worker exposure to conditions that lead to death or injury from violence by implementing effective security devices and administrative work practices, among other control measures.

The guidelines cover a broad spectrum of workers who provide health care and social services in psychiatric facilities, hospital emergency departments, community mental health clinics, drug abuse treatment clinics, pharmacies, community-care facilities and long-term care facilities. They include physicians, registered nurses, pharmacists, nurse practitioners, physicians' assistants, nurses' aides, therapists, technicians, public health nurses, home health care workers, social workers, welfare workers and emergency medical care personnel. The guidelines may also be useful in reducing risks for ancillary personnel such as maintenance, dietary, clerical and security staff in the health care and social service industries.

Violence Prevention Programs

A written program for job safety and security, incorporated into the organization's overall safety and health program, offers an effective approach for larger organizations. In smaller establishments, the program does not need to be written or heavily documented to be satisfactory.

What is needed are clear goals and objectives to prevent workplace violence suitable for the size and complexity of the workplace operation and adaptable to specific situations in each establishment. Employers should communicate information about the prevention program and startup date to all employees.

At a minimum, workplace violence prevention programs should:

- Create and disseminate a clear policy of zero tolerance for workplace violence, verbal and nonverbal threats and related actions. Ensure that managers, supervisors, coworkers, clients, patients and visitors know about this policy.

- Ensure that no employee who reports or experiences workplace violence faces reprisals.[6]

- Encourage employees to promptly report incidents and suggest ways to reduce or eliminate risks. Require records of incidents to assess risk and measure progress.

- Outline a comprehensive plan for maintaining security in the workplace. This includes establishing a liaison with law enforcement representatives and others who can help identify ways to prevent and mitigate workplace violence.

- Assign responsibility and authority for the program to individuals or teams with appropriate training and skills. Ensure that adequate resources are available for this effort and that the team or responsible individuals develop expertise on workplace violence prevention in health care and social services.

- Affirm management commitment to a worker-supportive environment that places as much importance on employee safety and health as on serving the patient or client.

- Set up a company briefing as part of the initial effort to address issues such as preserving safety, supporting affected employees and facilitating recovery.

Elements of an effective violence prevention program

The five main components of any effective safety and health program also apply to the prevention of workplace violence:

- Management commitment and employee involvement;
- Worksite analysis;
- Hazard prevention and control;
- Safety and health training; and
- Recordkeeping and program evaluation.

[6]Section 11 (c)(1) of the OSH Act applies to protected activity involving the hazard of workplace violence as it does for other health and safety matters:
"No person shall discharge or in any manner discriminate against any employee because such employee has filed any complaint or instituted or caused to be instituted any proceeding under or related to this Act or has testified or is about to testify in any such proceeding or because of the exercise by such employee on behalf of himself or others of any right afforded by this Act."

Management Commitment and Employee Involvement

Management commitment and employee involvement are complementary and essential elements of an effective safety and health program. To ensure an effective program, management and frontline employees must work together, perhaps through a team or committee approach. If employers opt for this strategy, they must be careful to comply with the applicable provisions of the *National Labor Relations Act.*[7]

Management commitment, including the endorsement and visible involvement of top management, provides the motivation and resources to deal effectively with workplace violence. This commitment should include:

- Demonstrating organizational concern for employee emotional and physical safety and health;
- Exhibiting equal commitment to the safety and health of workers and patients/clients;
- Assigning responsibility for the various aspects of the workplace violence prevention program to ensure that all managers, supervisors and employees understand their obligations;
- Allocating appropriate authority and resources to all responsible parties;
- Maintaining a system of accountability for involved managers, supervisors and employees;
- Establishing a comprehensive program of medical and psychological counseling and debriefing for employees experiencing or witnessing assaults and other violent incidents; and
- Supporting and implementing appropriate recommendations from safety and health committees.

Employee involvement and feedback enable workers to develop and express their own commitment to safety and health and provide useful information to design, implement and evaluate the program.

[7]29 U.S.C. 158(a)(2).

Employee involvement should include:

- Understanding and complying with the workplace violence prevention program and other safety and security measures;

- Participating in employee complaint or suggestion procedures covering safety and security concerns;

- Reporting violent incidents promptly and accurately;

- Participating in safety and health committees or teams that receive reports of violent incidents or security problems, make facility inspections and respond with recommendations for corrective strategies; and

- Taking part in a continuing education program that covers techniques to recognize escalating agitation, assaultive behavior or criminal intent and discusses appropriate responses.

Worksite Analysis
Value of a worksite analysis

A worksite analysis involves a step-by-step, commonsense look at the workplace to find existing or potential hazards for workplace violence. This entails reviewing specific procedures or operations that contribute to hazards and specific areas where hazards may develop. A threat assessment team, patient assault team, similar task force or coordinator may assess the vulnerability to workplace violence and determine the appropriate preventive actions to be taken. This group may also be responsible for implementing the workplace violence prevention program. The team should include representatives from senior management, operations, employee assistance, security, occupational safety and health, legal and human resources staff.

The team or coordinator can review injury and illness records and workers' compensation claims to identify patterns of assaults that could be prevented by workplace adaptation, procedural changes or employee training. As the team or coordinator identifies appropriate controls, they should be instituted.

Focus of a worksite analysis

The recommended program for worksite analysis includes, but is not limited to:

- Analyzing and tracking records;
- Screening surveys; and
- Analyzing workplace security.

Records analysis and tracking

This activity should include reviewing medical, safety, workers' compensation and insurance records—including the OSHA Log of Work-Related Injury and Illness (OSHA Form 300), if the employer is required to maintain one—to pinpoint instances of workplace violence. Scan unit logs and employee and police reports of incidents or near-incidents of assaultive behavior to identify and analyze trends in assaults relative to particular:

- Departments;
- Units;
- Job titles;
- Unit activities;
- Workstations; and
- Time of day.

Tabulate these data to target the frequency and severity of incidents to establish a baseline for measuring improvement. Monitor trends and analyze incidents. Contacting similar local businesses, trade associations and community and civic groups is one way to learn about their experiences with workplace violence and to help identify trends. Use several years of data, if possible, to trace trends of injuries and incidents of actual or potential workplace violence.

Value of screening surveys

One important screening tool is an employee questionnaire or survey to get employees' ideas on the potential for violent incidents and to identify or confirm the need for improved security measures. Detailed baseline screening surveys can help pinpoint tasks that put

employees at risk. Periodic surveys—conducted at least annually or whenever operations change or incidents of workplace violence occur—help identify new or previously unnoticed risk factors and deficiencies or failures in work practices, procedures or controls. Also, the surveys help assess the effects of changes in the work processes. The periodic review process should also include feedback and follow-up.

Independent reviewers, such as safety and health professionals, law enforcement or security specialists and insurance safety auditors, may offer advice to strengthen programs. These experts can also provide fresh perspectives to improve a violence prevention program.

Conducting a workplace security analysis

The team or coordinator should periodically inspect the workplace and evaluate employee tasks to identify hazards, conditions, operations and situations that could lead to violence.

To find areas requiring further evaluation, the team or coordinator should:

- Analyze incidents, including the characteristics of assailants and victims, an account of what happened before and during the incident, and the relevant details of the situation and its outcome. When possible, obtain police reports and recommendations.

- Identify jobs or locations with the greatest risk of violence as well as processes and procedures that put employees at risk of assault, including how often and when.

- Note high-risk factors such as types of clients or patients (for example, those with psychiatric conditions or who are disoriented by drugs, alcohol or stress); physical risk factors related to building layout or design; isolated locations and job activities; lighting problems; lack of phones and other communication devices; areas of easy, unsecured access; and areas with previous security problems.

- Evaluate the effectiveness of existing security measures, including engineering controls. Determine if risk factors have been reduced or eliminated and take appropriate action.

13

Hazard Prevention and Control

After hazards are identified through the systematic worksite analysis, the next step is to design measures through engineering or administrative and work practices to prevent or control these hazards. If violence does occur, post-incident response can be an important tool in preventing future incidents.

Engineering controls and workplace adaptations to minimize risk

Engineering controls remove the hazard from the workplace or create a barrier between the worker and the hazard. There are several measures that can effectively prevent or control workplace hazards, such as those described in the following paragraphs. The selection of any measure, of course, should be based on the hazards identified in the workplace security analysis of each facility.

Among other options, employers may choose to:

- Assess any plans for new construction or physical changes to the facility or workplace to eliminate or reduce security hazards.

- Install and regularly maintain alarm systems and other security devices, panic buttons, hand-held alarms or noise devices, cellular phones and private channel radios where risk is apparent or may be anticipated. Arrange for a reliable response system when an alarm is triggered.

- Provide metal detectors—installed or hand-held, where appropriate—to detect guns, knives or other weapons, according to the recommendations of security consultants.

- Use a closed-circuit video recording for high-risk areas on a 24-hour basis. Public safety is a greater concern than privacy in these situations.

- Place curved mirrors at hallway intersections or concealed areas.

- Enclose nurses' stations and install deep service counters or bullet-resistant, shatter-proof glass in reception, triage and admitting areas or client service rooms.

- Provide employee "safe rooms" for use during emergencies.

- Establish "time-out" or seclusion areas with high ceilings with-

out grids for patients who "act out" and establish separate rooms for criminal patients.

- Provide comfortable client or patient waiting rooms designed to minimize stress.
- Ensure that counseling or patient care rooms have two exits.
- Lock doors to staff counseling rooms and treatment rooms to limit access.
- Arrange furniture to prevent entrapment of staff.
- Use minimal furniture in interview rooms or crisis treatment areas and ensure that it is lightweight, without sharp corners or edges and affixed to the floor, if possible. Limit the number of pictures, vases, ashtrays or other items that can be used as weapons.
- Provide lockable and secure bathrooms for staff members separate from patient/client and visitor facilities.
- Lock all unused doors to limit access, in accordance with local fire codes.
- Install bright, effective lighting, both indoors and outdoors.
- Replace burned-out lights and broken windows and locks.
- Keep automobiles well maintained if they are used in the field.
- Lock automobiles at all times.

Administrative and work practice controls to minimize risk

Administrative and work practice controls affect the way staff perform jobs or tasks. Changes in work practices and administrative procedures can help prevent violent incidents. Some options for employers are to:

- State clearly to patients, clients and employees that violence is not permitted or tolerated.
- Establish liaison with local police and state prosecutors. Report all incidents of violence. Give police physical layouts of facilities to expedite investigations.
- Require employees to report all assaults or threats to a supervisor or manager (for example, through a confidential interview). Keep log books and reports of such incidents to help determine any necessary actions to prevent recurrences.

15

- Advise employees of company procedures for requesting police assistance or filing charges when assaulted and help them do so, if necessary.

- Provide management support during emergencies. Respond promptly to all complaints.

- Set up a trained response team to respond to emergencies.

- Use properly trained security officers to deal with aggressive behavior. Follow written security procedures.

- Ensure that adequate and properly trained staff are available to restrain patients or clients, if necessary.

- Provide sensitive and timely information to people waiting in line or in waiting rooms. Adopt measures to decrease waiting time.

- Ensure that adequate and qualified staff are available at all times. The times of greatest risk occur during patient transfers, emergency responses, mealtimes and at night. Areas with the greatest risk include admission units and crisis or acute care units.

- Institute a sign-in procedure with passes for visitors, especially in a newborn nursery or pediatric department. Enforce visitor hours and procedures.

- Establish a list of "restricted visitors" for patients with a history of violence or gang activity. Make copies available at security checkpoints, nurses' stations and visitor sign-in areas.

- Review and revise visitor check systems, when necessary. Limit information given to outsiders about hospitalized victims of violence.

- Supervise the movement of psychiatric clients and patients throughout the facility.

- Control access to facilities other than waiting rooms, particularly drug storage or pharmacy areas.

- Prohibit employees from working alone in emergency areas or walk-in clinics, particularly at night or when assistance is unavailable. Do not allow employees to enter seclusion rooms alone.

- Establish policies and procedures for secured areas and emergency evacuations.

- Determine the behavioral history of new and transferred patients to learn about any past violent or assaultive behaviors.

- Establish a system—such as chart tags, log books or verbal census reports—to identify patients and clients with assaultive behavior problems. Keep in mind patient confidentiality and worker safety issues. Update as needed.

- Treat and interview aggressive or agitated clients in relatively open areas that still maintain privacy and confidentiality (such as rooms with removable partitions).

- Use case management conferences with coworkers and supervisors to discuss ways to effectively treat potentially violent patients.

- Prepare contingency plans to treat clients who are "acting out" or making verbal or physical attacks or threats. Consider using certified employee assistance professionals or in-house social service or occupational health service staff to help diffuse patient or client anger.

- Transfer assaultive clients to acute care units, criminal units or other more restrictive settings.

- Ensure that nurses and physicians are not alone when performing intimate physical examinations of patients.

- Discourage employees from wearing necklaces or chains to help prevent possible strangulation in confrontational situations. Urge community workers to carry only required identification and money.

- Survey the facility periodically to remove tools or possessions left by visitors or maintenance staff that could be used inappropriately by patients.

- Provide staff with identification badges, preferably without last names, to readily verify employment.

- Discourage employees from carrying keys, pens or other items that could be used as weapons.

- Provide staff members with security escorts to parking areas in evening or late hours. Ensure that parking areas are highly visible, well lit and safely accessible to the building.

- Use the "buddy system," especially when personal safety may be threatened. Encourage home health care providers, social service workers and others to avoid threatening situations.

- Advise staff to exercise extra care in elevators, stairwells and unfamiliar residences; leave the premises immediately if there is a hazardous situation; or request police escort if needed.

- Develop policies and procedures covering home health care providers, such as contracts on how visits will be conducted, the presence of others in the home during the visits and the refusal to provide services in a clearly hazardous situation.

- Establish a daily work plan for field staff to keep a designated contact person informed about their whereabouts throughout the workday. Have the contact person follow up if an employee does not report in as expected.

Employer responses to incidents of violence

Post-incident response and evaluation are essential to an effective violence prevention program. All workplace violence programs should provide comprehensive treatment for employees who are victimized personally or may be traumatized by witnessing a workplace violence incident. Injured staff should receive prompt treatment and psychological evaluation whenever an assault takes place, regardless of its severity. Provide the injured transportation to medical care if it is not available onsite.

Victims of workplace violence suffer a variety of consequences in addition to their actual physical injuries. These may include:

- Short- and long-term psychological trauma;

- Fear of returning to work;

- Changes in relationships with coworkers and family;

- Feelings of incompetence, guilt, powerlessness; and

- Fear of criticism by supervisors or managers.

Consequently, a strong follow-up program for these employees will not only help them to deal with these problems but also help prepare them to confront or prevent future incidents of violence.

Several types of assistance can be incorporated into the post-incident response. For example, trauma-crisis counseling, critical-incident stress debriefing or employee assistance programs may be provided to assist victims. Certified employee assistance professionals, psychologists, psychiatrists, clinical nurse specialists

or social workers may provide this counseling or the employer may refer staff victims to an outside specialist. In addition, the employer may establish an employee counseling service, peer counseling or support groups.

Counselors should be well trained and have a good understanding of the issues and consequences of assaults and other aggressive, violent behavior. Appropriate and promptly rendered post-incident debriefings and counseling reduce acute psychological trauma and general stress levels among victims and witnesses. In addition, this type of counseling educates staff about workplace violence and positively influences workplace and organizational cultural norms to reduce trauma associated with future incidents.

Safety and Health Training

Training and education ensure that all staff are aware of potential security hazards and how to protect themselves and their coworkers through established policies and procedures.

Training for all employees

Every employee should understand the concept of "universal precautions for violence" — that is, that violence should be expected but can be avoided or mitigated through preparation. Frequent training also can reduce the likelihood of being assaulted.

Employees who may face safety and security hazards should receive formal instruction on the specific hazards associated with the unit or job and facility. This includes information on the types of injuries or problems identified in the facility and the methods to control the specific hazards. It also includes instructions to limit physical interventions in workplace altercations whenever possible, unless enough staff or emergency response teams and security personnel are available. In addition, all employees should be trained to behave compassionately toward coworkers when an incident occurs.

The training program should involve all employees, including supervisors and managers.

New and reassigned employees should receive an initial orientation before being assigned their job duties. Visiting staff, such as physicians, should receive the same training as permanent staff. Qualified trainers should instruct at the comprehension level

appropriate for the staff. Effective training programs should involve role playing, simulations and drills.

Topics may include management of 'assaultive behavior, professional assault-response training, police assault-avoidance programs or personal safety training such as how to prevent and avoid assaults. A combination of training programs may be used, depending on the severity of the risk.

Employees should receive required training annually. In large institutions, refresher programs may be needed more frequently, perhaps monthly or quarterly, to effectively reach and inform all employees.

What training should cover

The training should cover topics such as:

- The workplace violence prevention policy;
- Risk factors that cause or contribute to assaults;
- Early recognition of escalating behavior or recognition of warning signs or situations that may lead to assaults;
- Ways to prevent or diffuse volatile situations or aggressive behavior, manage anger and appropriately use medications as chemical restraints;
- A standard response action plan for violent situations, including the availability of assistance, response to alarm systems and communication procedures;
- Ways to deal with hostile people other than patients and clients, such as relatives and visitors;
- Progressive behavior control methods and safe methods to apply restraints;
- The location and operation of safety devices such as alarm systems, along with the required maintenance schedules and procedures;
- Ways to protect oneself and coworkers, including use of the "buddy system;"
- Policies and procedures for reporting and recordkeeping;
- Information on multicultural diversity to increase staff sensitivity to racial and ethnic issues and differences; and

- Policies and procedures for obtaining medical care, counseling, workers' compensation or legal assistance after a violent episode or injury.

Training for supervisors and managers

Supervisors and managers need to learn to recognize high-risk situations, so they can ensure that employees are not placed in assignments that compromise their safety. They also need training to ensure that they encourage employees to report incidents.

Supervisors and managers should learn how to reduce security hazards and ensure that employees receive appropriate training. Following training, supervisors and managers should be able to recognize a potentially hazardous situation and to make any necessary changes in the physical plant, patient care treatment program and staffing policy and procedures to reduce or eliminate the hazards.

Training for security personnel

Security personnel need specific training from the hospital or clinic, including the psychological components of handling aggressive and abusive clients, types of disorders and ways to handle aggression and defuse hostile situations.

The training program should also include an evaluation. At least annually, the team or coordinator responsible for the program should review its content, methods and the frequency of training. Program evaluation may involve supervisor and employee interviews, testing and observing and reviewing reports of behavior of individuals in threatening situations.

Recordkeeping and Program Evaluation
How employers can determine program effectiveness

Recordkeeping and evaluation of the violence prevention program are necessary to determine its overall effectiveness and identify any deficiencies or changes that should be made.

Records employers should keep

Recordkeeping is essential to the program's success. Good records help employers determine the severity of the problem,

evaluate methods of hazard control and identify training needs. Records can be especially useful to large organizations and for members of a business group or trade association who "pool" data. Records of injuries, illnesses, accidents, assaults, hazards, corrective actions, patient histories and training can help identify problems and solutions for an effective program.

Important Records:
- OSHA Log of Work-Related Injury and Illness (OSHA Form 300). Employers who are required to keep this log must record any new work-related injury that results in death, days away from work, days of restriction or job transfer, medical treatment beyond first aid, loss of consciousness or a significant injury diagnosed by a licensed health care professional. Injuries caused by assaults must be entered on the log if they meet the recording criteria. All employers must report, within 24 hours, a fatality or an incident that results in the hospitalization of three or more employees.[8]

- Medical reports of work injury and supervisors' reports for each recorded assault. These records should describe the type of assault, such as an unprovoked sudden attack or patient-to-patient altercation; who was assaulted; and all other circumstances of the incident. The records should include a description of the environment or location, potential or actual cost, lost work time that resulted and the nature of injuries sustained. These medical records are confidential documents and should be kept in a locked location under the direct responsibility of a health care professional.

- Records of incidents of abuse, verbal attacks or aggressive behavior that may be threatening, such as pushing or shouting and acts of aggression toward other clients. This may be kept as part of an assaultive incident report. Ensure that the affected department evaluates these records routinely. (See sample violence incident forms in Appendix B.)

- Information on patients with a history of past violence, drug abuse or criminal activity recorded on the patient's chart. All staff who care for a potentially aggressive, abusive or violent client

[8] 29 CFR Part 1904, revised 2001.

22

should be aware of the person's background and history. Log the admission of violent patients to help determine potential risks.

- Documentation of minutes of safety meetings, records of hazard analyses and corrective actions recommended and taken.
- Records of all training programs, attendees and qualifications of trainers.

Elements of a program evaluation

As part of their overall program, employers should evaluate their safety and security measures. Top management should review the program regularly, and with each incident, to evaluate its success. Responsible parties (including managers, supervisors and employees) should reevaluate policies and procedures on a regular basis to identify deficiencies and take corrective action.

Management should share workplace violence prevention evaluation reports with all employees. Any changes in the program should be discussed at regular meetings of the safety committee, union representatives or other employee groups.

All reports should protect employee confidentiality either by presenting only aggregate data or by removing personal identifiers if individual data are used.

Processes involved in an evaluation include:
- Establishing a uniform violence reporting system and regular review of reports;
- Reviewing reports and minutes from staff meetings on safety and security issues;
- Analyzing trends and rates in illnesses, injuries or fatalities caused by violence relative to initial or "baseline" rates;
- Measuring improvement based on lowering the frequency and severity of workplace violence;
- Keeping up-to-date records of administrative and work practice changes to prevent workplace violence to evaluate how well they work;
- Surveying employees before and after making job or worksite changes or installing security measures or new systems to determine their effectiveness;

- Keeping abreast of new strategies available to deal with violence in the health care and social service fields as they develop;

- Surveying employees periodically to learn if they experience hostile situations concerning the medical treatment they provide;

- Complying with OSHA and State requirements for recording and reporting deaths, injuries and illnesses; and

- Requesting periodic law enforcement or outside consultant review of the worksite for recommendations on improving employee safety.

Sources of assistance for employers

Employers who would like help in implementing an appropriate workplace violence prevention program can turn to the OSHA Consultation Service provided in their State. To contact this service, see OSHA's website at www.osha.gov or call (800) 321-OSHA.

OSHA's efforts to help employers combat workplace violence are complemented by those of NIOSH, public safety officials, trade associations, unions, insurers and human resource and employee assistance professionals, as well as other interested groups. Employers and employees may contact these groups for additional advice and information. NIOSH can be reached toll-free at (800) 35-NIOSH.

Conclusion

OSHA recognizes the importance of effective safety and health program management in providing safe and healthful workplaces. Effective safety and health programs improve both morale and productivity and reduce workers' compensation costs.

OSHA's violence prevention guidelines are an essential component of workplace safety and health programs. OSHA believes the performance-oriented approach of these guidelines provides employers with flexibility in their efforts to maintain safe and healthful working conditions.

References

California State Department of Industrial Relations, Cal/OSHA. (1998). *Guidelines for Security and Safety of Health Care and Community Service Workers*. www.dir.ca.gov/dosh/dosh%5Fpublications/hcworker.html

Centers for Disease Control and Prevention, National Institute for Occupational Health. (2002). *Occupational Hazards in Hospitals*. DHHS (NIOSH) Pub. No. 2002-101. www.cdc.gov/niosh/2002-101.html

U.S. Department of Justice, Bureau of Justice Statistics. (2001). *National Crime Victimization Survey. Violence in the Workplace, 1993–99*. www.ojp.gov/bjs/pub/pdf/vw99.pdf

U.S. Department of Labor, Bureau of Labor Statistics. (2002). *Census of Fatal Occupational Injuries, 2001*. www.bls.gov/iif/oshwc/cfoi/cfnr0008.pdf

U.S. Department of Labor, Bureau of Labor Statistics. (2001). Survey of Occupational Injuries and Illnesses, 2000. www.bls.gov/iif/oshwc/osh/os/osnr0013.pdf

Washington, Department of Labor and Industries. Workplace Violence: *Awareness and Prevention for Employers and Employees, 2000*. www.lni.wa.gov/ipub/417-140-000.htm

OSHA assistance

OSHA can provide extensive help through a variety of programs, including technical assistance about effective safety and health programs, state plans, workplace consultations, voluntary protection programs, strategic partnerships, training and education and more. An overall commitment to workplace safety and health can add value to your business, to your workplace and to your life.

Safety and Health Program Management Guidelines

Effective management of worker safety and health protection is a decisive factor in reducing the extent and severity of work-related injuries and illnesses and their related costs. In fact, an effective safety and health program forms the basis of good worker protection and can save time and money (about $4 for every dollar

spent) and increase productivity and reduce worker injuries, illnesses and related workers' compensation costs.

To assist employers and employees in developing effective safety and health programs, OSHA published recommended *Safety and Health Program Management Guidelines* (54 *Federal Register* (16): 3904-3916, January 26, 1989). These voluntary guidelines apply to all places of employment covered by OSHA.

The guidelines identify four general elements critical to the development of a successful safety and health management program:

- Management leadership and employee involvement.
- Work analysis.
- Hazard prevention and control.
- Safety and health training.

The guidelines recommend specific actions, under each of these general elements, to achieve an effective safety and health program. The *Federal Register* notice is available online at www.osha.gov.

State Programs

The Occupational Safety and Health Act of 1970 (*OSH Act*) encourages states to develop and operate their own job safety and health plans. OSHA approves and monitors these plans. There are currently 26 state plans: 23 cover both private and public (state and local government) employment; 3 states, Connecticut, New Jersey and New York, cover the public sector only. States and territories with their own OSHA-approved occupational safety and health plans must adopt standards identical to, or at least as effective as, the federal standards.

Consultation Services

Consultation assistance is available on request to employers who want help in establishing and maintaining a safe and healthful workplace. Largely funded by OSHA, the service is provided at no cost to the employer. Primarily developed for smaller employers with more hazardous operations, the consultation service is de-livered by state governments employing professional safety and health consultants. Comprehensive assistance includes an appraisal of all-mechanical systems, work practices and occupational safety

and health hazards of the workplace and all aspects of the employer's present job safety and health program. In addition, the service offers assistance to employers in developing and implementing an effective safety and health program. No penalties are proposed or citations issued for hazards identified by the consultant. OSHA provides consultation assistance to the employer with the assurance that his or her name and firm and any information about the workplace will not be routinely reported to OSHA enforcement staff.

Under the consultation program, certain exemplary employers may request participation in OSHA's Safety and Health Achievement Recognition Program (SHARP). Eligibility for participation in SHARP includes receiving a comprehensive consultation visit, demonstrating exemplary achievements in workplace safety and health by abating all identified hazards and developing an excellent safety and health program.

Employers accepted into SHARP may receive an exemption from programmed inspections (not complaint or accident investigation inspections) for a period of one year. For more information concerning consultation assistance, see the OSHA website at www.osha.gov.

Voluntary Protection Programs (VPP)

Voluntary Protection Programs and onsite consultation services, when coupled with an effective enforcement program, expand worker protection to help meet the goals of the *OSH Act*. The three levels of VPP are Star, Merit, and Demonstration designed to recognize outstanding achievements by companies that have successfully incorporated comprehensive safety and health programs into their total management system. The VPPs motivate others to achieve excellent safety and health results in the same outstanding way as they establish a cooperative relationship between employers, employees and OSHA.

For additional information on VPP and how to apply, contact the OSHA regional offices listed at the end of this publication.

Strategic Partnership Program

OSHA's Strategic Partnership Program, the newest member of OSHA's cooperative programs, helps encourage, assist and recognize the efforts of partners to eliminate serious workplace

hazards and achieve a high level of worker safety and health. Whereas OSHA's Consultation Program and VPP entail one-on-one relationships between OSHA and individual worksites, most strategic partnerships seek to have a broader impact by building cooperative relationships with groups of employers and employees. These partnerships are voluntary, cooperative relationships between OSHA, employers, employee representatives and others (e.g., trade unions, trade and professional associations, universities and other government agencies).

For more information on this and other cooperative programs, contact your nearest OSHA office, or visit OSHA's website at www.osha.gov.

Alliance Programs

The Alliances Program enables organizations committed to workplace safety and health to collaborate with OSHA to prevent injuries and illnesses in the workplace. OSHA and the Alliance participants work together to reach out to, educate and lead the nation's employers and their employees in improving and advancing workplace safety and health.

Alliances are open to all groups, including trade or professional organizations, businesses, labor organizations, educational institutions and government agencies. In some cases, organizations may be building on existing relationships with OSHA that were developed through other cooperative programs.

There are few formal program requirements for Alliances and the agreements do not include an enforcement component. However, OSHA and the participating organizations must define, implement and meet a set of short- and long-term goals that fall into three categories: training and education; outreach and communication; and promoting the national dialogue on workplace safety and health.

OSHA Training and Education

OSHA area offices offer a variety of information services, such as compliance assistance, technical advice, publications, audiovisual aids and speakers for special engagements. OSHA's Training Institute in Arlington Heights, Ill., provides basic and advanced courses in safety and health for federal and state compliance officers, state consultants, federal agency personnel, and private

sector employers, employees and their representatives.

The OSHA Training Institute also has established OSHA Training Institute Education Centers to address the increased demand for its courses from the private sector and from other federal agencies. These centers are nonprofit colleges, universities and other organizations that have been selected after a competition for participation in the program.

OSHA also provides funds to nonprofit organizations, through grants, to conduct workplace training and education in subjects where OSHA believes there is a lack of workplace training. Grants are awarded annually. Grant recipients are expected to contribute 20 percent of the total grant cost.

For more information on grants, training and education, contact the OSHA Training Institute, Office of Training and Education, 2020 South Arlington Heights Road, Arlington Heights, IL 60005, (847) 297-4810 or see "Outreach" on OSHA's website at www.osha.gov. For further information on any OSHA program, contact your nearest OSHA area or regional office listed at the end of this publication.

Information Available Electronically

OSHA has a variety of materials and tools available on its website at www.osha.gov. These include *e-Tools* such as *Expert Advisors, Electronic Compliance Assistance Tools (e-cats), Technical Links*; regulations, directives and publications; videos and other information for employers and employees. OSHA's software programs and compliance assistance tools walk you through challenging safety and health issues and common problems to find the best solutions for your workplace.

OSHA's CD-ROM includes standards, interpretations, directives and more, and can be purchased on CD-ROM from the U.S. Government Printing Office. To order, write to the Superintendent of Documents, P.O. Box 371954, Pittsburgh, PA 15250-7954 or phone (202) 512-1800, or order online at http://bookstore.gpo.gov.

OSHA Publications

OSHA has an extensive publications program. For a listing of free or sales items, visit OSHA's website at www.osha.gov or contact the OSHA Publications Office, U.S. Department of Labor, 200 Constitution Avenue, NW, N-3101, Washington, DC 20210. Telephone (202) 693-1888 or fax to (202) 693-2498.

Contacting OSHA

To report an emergency, file a complaint or seek OSHA advice, assistance or products, call (800) 321-OSHA or contact your nearest OSHA regional or area office listed at the end of this publication. The teletypewriter (TTY) number is (877) 889-5627.

You can also file a complaint online and obtain more information on OSHA federal and state programs by visiting OSHA's website at www.osha.gov.

OSHA Regional Offices

Region I
(CT,* ME, MA, NH, RI, VT*)
JFK Federal Building, Room E340
Boston, MA 02203
(617) 565-9860

Region II
(NJ,* NY,* PR,* VI*)
201 Varick Street, Room 670
New York, NY 10014
(212) 337-2378

Region III
(DE, DC, MD,* PA,* VA,* WV)
The Curtis Center
170 S. Independence Mall West
Suite 740 West
Philadelphia, PA 19106-3309
(215) 861-4900

Region IV
(AL, FL, GA, KY,* MS, NC,* SC,* TN*)
61 Forsyth Street, SW
Atlanta, GA 30303
(404) 562-2300

Region V
(IL, IN,* MI,* MN,* OH, WI)
230 South Dearborn Street, Room 3244
Chicago, IL 60604
(312) 353-2220

Region VI
(AR, LA, NM,* OK, TX)
525 Griffin Street, Room 602
Dallas, TX 75202
(214) 767-4731 or 4736 x224

Region VII
(IA,* KS, MO, NE)
City Center Square
1100 Main Street, Suite 800
Kansas City, MO 64105
(816) 426-5861

Region VIII
(CO, MT, ND, SD, UT,* WY*)
1999 Broadway, Suite 1690
PO Box 46550
Denver, CO 80201-6550
(303) 844-1600

Region IX
(American Samoa, AZ,* CA,* HI, NV,* Northern Mariana Islands)
71 Stevenson Street, Room 420
San Francisco, CA 94105
(415) 975-4310

Region X
(AK,* ID, OR,* WA*)
1111 Third Avenue, Suite 715
Seattle, WA 98101-3212
(206) 553-5930

*These states and territories operate their own OSHA-approved job safety and health programs (Connecticut, New Jersey and New York plans cover public employees only). States with approved programs must have a standard that is identical to, or at least as effective as, the federal standard.

Note: To get contact information for OSHA Area Offices, OSHA-approved State Plans and OSHA Consultation Projects, please visit us online at www.osha.gov or call us at 1-800-321-OSHA.

Appendix A:
Workplace Violence Program Checklists

Reprinted with permission of the American Nurses Association, Promoting Safe Work Environments for Nurses, 2002.

Checklist 1:
Organizational Assessment Questions Regarding Management Commitment and Employee Involvement

- Is there demonstrated organizational concern for employee emotional and physical safety and health as well as that of the patients?

- Is there a written workplace violence prevention program in your facility?

- Did front-line workers as well as management participate in developing the plan?

- Is there someone clearly responsible for the violence prevention program to ensure that all managers, supervisors, and employees understand their obligations?

- Do those responsible have sufficient authority and resources to take all action necessary to ensure worker safety?

- Does the violence prevention program address the kinds of violent incidents that are occurring in your facility?

- Does the program provide for post-assault medical treatment and psychological counseling for health-care workers who experience or witness assaults or violence incidents?

- Is there a system to notify employees promptly about specific workplace security hazards or threats that are made? Are employees aware of this system?

- Is there a system for employees to inform management about workplace security hazards or threats without fear of reprisal? Are employees aware of this system?

- Is there a system for employees to promptly report violent incidents, "near misses," threats, and verbal assaults without fear of reprisal?

- Is there tracking, trending, and regular reporting on violent incidents through the safety committee?

- Are front-line workers included as regular members and partici-pants in the safety committee as well as violence tracking activities?

- Does the tracking and reporting capture all types of violence— fatalities, physical assaults, harassment, aggressive behavior, threats, verbal abuse, and sexual assaults?

- Does the tracking and reporting system use the latest categories of violence so data can be compared?

- Have the high-risk locations or jobs with the greatest risk of violence as well as the processes and procedures that put employees at risk been identified?

- Is there a root-cause analysis of the risk factors associated with individual violent incidents so that current response systems can be addressed and hazards can be eliminated and corrected?

- Are employees consulted about what corrective actions need to be taken for single incidents or surveyed about violence concerns in general?

- Is there follow-up of employees involved in or witnessing violent incidents to assure that appropriate medical treatment and counseling have been provided?

- Has a process for reporting violent incidents within the facility to the police or requesting police assistance been established?

Identifying Risks for Violence by Unit/Work Area

Perform a step-by-step review of each work area to identify specific places and times that violent incidents are occurring and the risk factors that are present. To ensure multiple perspectives, it is best for a team to perform this worksite analysis. Key members of the analysis team should be front-line health care workers, including nurses from each specialty unit, as well as the facility's safety and security professionals.

Find Out What's Happening on Paper

The first step in this worksite analysis is to obtain and review data that tells the "who, what, when, where and why" about violent incidents. These sources include:

- Incident report forms
- Workers' compensation reports of injury

- OSHA 300 injury and illness logs
- Security logs
- Reports to police
- Safety committee reports
- Hazard inspection reports
- Staff termination records
- Union complaints

Using this information, attempt to answer the questions in Checklist 2.

Checklist 2:
Analyze Workplace Violence Records

- How many incidents occurred in the last 2 years?
- What kinds of incidents occurred most often (assault, threats, robbery, vandalism, etc.)?
- Where did incidents most often occur?
- When did incidents most often occur (day of week, shift, time, etc.)?
- What job task was usually being performed when an incident occurred?
- Which workers were victimized most often (gender, age, job classification, etc.)?
- What type of weapon was used most often?
- Are there any similarities among the assailants?
- What other incidents, if any, are you aware of that are not included in the records?
- Of those incidents you reviewed, which one or two were most serious?

Use the data collected to stimulate the following discussions:

- Are there any important patterns or trends among the incidents?
- What do you believe were the main factors contributing to violence in your workplace?

- What additional corrective measures would you recommend to reduce or eliminate the problems you identified?

Conduct a Walkthrough

It is important to keep in mind that injuries from violence are often not reported. One of the best ways to observe what is really going on is to conduct a workplace walkthrough.

A walkthrough, which is really a workplace inspection, is the first step in identifying violence risk factors and serves several important functions. While on a walkthrough, hazards can be recognized and often corrected before anyone's health and safety is affected.

While inspecting for workplace violence risk factors, review the physical facility and note the presence or absence of security measures. Local police may also be able to conduct a security audit or provide information about experience with crime in the area.

Ask the Workers

A simple survey can provide valuable information often not found in department walkthroughs and injury logs. Some staff may not report violent acts or threatening situations formally but will share the experiences and suggestions anonymously. This can provide information about previously unnoticed deficiencies or failures in work practices or administrative controls. It also can help increase employee awareness about dangerous conditions and encourage them to become involved in prevention activities.

Types of questions that employees should be asked include:

- What do they see as risk factors for violence?

  - The most important risk factors in their work areas
  - Aspects of the physical environment that contribute to violence
  - Dangerous situations or "near misses" experienced
  - Assault experiences—past year, entire time at facility
  - Staffing adequacy

- How are current control measures working?

  - Hospital practices for handling conflict among staff and patients
  - Effectiveness of response to violent incidents

- How safe they feel in the current environment

- What ideas do employees have to protect workers?
  - Highest priorities in violence prevention
  - Ideas for improvements and prevention measures

- How satisfied are they in their jobs?
  - With managers/fellow workers
  - Adequacy of rewards and praise
  - Impact on health

Checklist 3:
Identifying Environmental Risk Factors for Violence

Use the following checklist to assist in your workplace walkthrough.

General questions about approach:
- Are safety and security issues specifically considered in the early stages of facility design, construction, and renovation?
- Does the current violence prevention program provide a way to select and implement controls based on the specific risks identified in the workplace security analysis? How does this process occur?

Specific questions about the environment:
- Do crime patterns in the neighborhood influence safety in the facility?
- Do workers feel safe walking to and from the workplace?
- Are entrances visible to security personnel and are they well lit and free of hiding places?
- Is there adequate security in parking or public transit waiting areas?
- Is public access to the building controlled, and is this system effective?
- Can exit doors be opened only from the inside to prevent unauthorized entry?

- Is there an internal phone system to activate emergency assistance?

- Have alarm systems or panic buttons been installed in high-risk areas?

- Given the history of violence at the facility, is a metal detector appropriate in some entry areas? Closed-circuit TV in high-risk areas?

- Is there good lighting?

- Are fire exits and escape routes clearly marked?

- Are reception and work areas designed to prevent unauthorized entry? Do they provide staff good visibility of patients and visitors? If not, are there other provisions such as security cameras or mirrors?

- Are patient or client areas designed to minimize stress, including minimizing noise?

- Are drugs, equipment, and supplies adequately secured?

- Is there a secure place for employees to store their belongings?

- Are "safe rooms" available for staff use during emergencies?

- Are door locks in patient rooms appropriate? Can they be opened during an emergency?

- Do counseling or patient care rooms have two exits, and is furniture arranged to prevent employees from becoming trapped?

- Are lockable and secure bathrooms that are separate from patient-client and visitor facilities available for staff members?

Checklist 4:
Assessing the Influence of Day-to-Day Work Practices on Occurrences of Violence

- Are identification tags required for both employees and visitors to the building?

- Is there a way to identify patients with a history of violence? Are contingency plans put in place for these patients—such as restricting visitors and supervising their movement through the facility?

- Are emergency phone numbers and procedures posted or readily available?

- Are there trained security personnel accessible to workers in a timely manner?
- Are waiting times for patients kept as short as possible to avoid frustration?
- Is there adequate and qualified staffing at all times, particularly during patient transfers, emergency responses, mealtimes, and at night?
- Are employees prohibited from entering seclusion rooms alone or working alone in emergency areas of walk-in clinics, particularly at night or when assistance is unavailable?
- Are broken windows, doors, locks, and lights replaced promptly?
- Are security alarms and devices tested regularly?

Checklist 5:
Post-Incident Response

- Is comprehensive treatment provided to victimized employees as well as those who may be traumatized by witnessing a workplace violence incident? Required services may include trauma-crisis counseling, critical incident stress debriefing, psychological counseling services, peer counseling, and support groups.

Checklist 6:
Assessing Employee and Supervisor Training

- Does the violence prevention program require training for all employees and supervisors when they are hired and when job responsibilities change?
- Do agency workers or contract physicians and house staff receive the same training that permanent staff receive?
- Are workers trained in how to handle difficult clients or patients?
- Does the security staff receive specialized training for the health-care environment?
- Is the training tailored to specific units, patient populations, and job tasks, including any tasks done in the field?
- Do employees learn progressive behavior control methods and safe methods to apply restraints?

- Do workers believe that the training is effective in handling escalating violence or violent incidents?
- Are drills conducted to test the response of health-care facility personnel?
- Are workers trained in how to report violent incidents, threats, or abuse and obtain medical care, counseling, workers' compensation, or legal assistance after a violent episode or injury?
- Are employees and supervisors trained to behave compassionately toward coworkers when an incident occurs?
- Does the training include instruction about the location and operation of safety devices such as alarm systems, along with the required maintenance schedules and procedures?

Checklist 7:
Recordkeeping and Evaluation

Does the violence prevention program provide for:

- Up-to-date recording in the OSHA Log of Work-Related Injury and Illness (OSHA 300)?
- Records of all incidents involving assault, harassment, aggressive behavior, abuse, and verbal attack with attention to maintaining appropriate confidentiality of the records?
- Training records?
- Workplace walkthrough and security inspection records?
- Keeping records of control measures instituted in response to inspections, complaints, or violent incidents?
- A system for regular evaluation of engineering, administrative, and work practice controls to see if they are working well?
- A system for regular review of individual reports and trending and analysis of all incidents?
- Employee surveys regarding the effectiveness of control measures instituted?
- Discussions with employees who are involved in hostile situations to ask about the quality of post-incident treatment they received?
- A provision for an outside audit or consultation of the violence programs for recommendations on improving safety?

Appendix B
Violence Incident Report Forms

Sample 1

The following items serve merely as an example of what might be used or modified by employers in these industries to help prevent workplace violence. (Sample/Draft—Adapt to your own location and business circumstances.)

Confidential Incident Report

To:_____ Date of Incident:_____

Location of Incident *(Map/sketch on reverse side or attached)*:_____

From:_____ Phone:_____ Time of Incident:_____

Nature of the Incident (*"X" all applicable boxes*):
- ❑ Assaults or Violent Acts:____Type "1"____Type "2"____Type "3"____Other
- ❑ Preventative or Warning Report
- ❑ Bomb or Terrorist Type Threat ❑ Yes ❑ No
- ❑ Transportation Accident ❑ Contacts with Objects or Equipment
- ❑ Falls ❑ Exposures ❑ Fires or Explosions ❑ Other

Legal Counsel Advised of Incident? ❑ Yes ❑ No EAP Advised? ❑ Yes ❑ No
Warning or Preventative Measures? ❑ Yes ❑ No
Number of Persons Affected:_____

(*For each person, complete a report; however, to the extent facts are duplicative, any person's report may incorporate another person's report.*)

Name of Affected Person(s):_____ Service Date:_____
Position:_____ Member of Labor Organization? ❑ Yes ❑ No
Supervisor:_____ Has Supervisor Been Notified? ❑ Yes ❑ No
Family:_____ Has Been Notified by:_____? ❑ Yes ❑ No
Lost Work Time? ❑ Yes ❑ No Anticipated Return to Work:_____
Third parties or non-employee involvement (*include contractor and lease employees, visitors, vendors, customers*)? ❑ Yes ❑ No

Nature of the Incident

Briefly describe: (1) event(s); (2) witnesses with addresses and status included; (3) location details; (4) equipment/weapon details; (5) weather; (6) other records of the incident (e.g., police report, recordings, videos); (7) the ability to observe and reliability of witnesses; (8) were the parties possibly impaired because of illness, injury, drugs or alcohol? (were tests taken to verify same?); (9) parties notified internally (employee relations, medical, legal, operations, etc.) and externally (police, fire, ambulance, EAP, family, etc.).

Previous or Related Incidents of This Type? ❑ Yes ❑ No
Or by This Person? ❑ Yes ❑ No Preventative Steps? ❑ Yes ❑ No
OSHA Log or Other OSHA Action Required? ❑ Yes ❑ No
Incident Response Team:_____

Team Leader:_____ _____
                       Signature   *Date*

Source: Reprinted with permission of Karen Smith Keinbaum, Esq., Counsel to the Law Firm of Abbott, Nicholson, Quilter, Esshaki & Youngblood, P. C., Detroit, MI.

Sample 2

The following items serve merely as an example of what might be used or modified by employers in these industries to help prevent workplace violence.

A reportable violent incident should be defined as any threatening remark or overt act of physical violence against a person(s) or property whether reported or observed.

1. Date:_____ Day of Week: _____ Time:_____ Assailant: ❑ Female ❑ Male

2. Specific Location: _____

3. Violence Directed Toward: ❑ Patient ❑ Staff ❑ Visitor ❑ Other
Assailant: ❑ Patient ❑ Staff ❑ Visitor ❑ Other
Assailant's Name:_____
Assailant: ❑ Unarmed ❑ Armed (weapon)

4. Predisposing Factors:
❑ Intoxication ❑ Dissatisfied with Care/Waiting Time
❑ Grief Reaction ❑ Prior History of Violence
❑ Gang Related ❑ Other (Describe) _____

5. Description of Incident: ❑ Physical Abuse ❑ Verbal Abuse ❑ Other

6. Injuries: ❑ Yes ❑ No

7. Extent of Injuries:_____

8. Detailed Description of the Incident: _____

9. Did Any Person Leave the Area because of Incident?
❑ Yes ❑ No ❑ Unable to Determine

10. Present at Time of Incident:
❑ Police Name of Department:_____
❑ Hospital Security Officer

11. Needed to Call:
❑ Police Name of Department:_____
❑ Hospital Security

12. Termination of Incident:
Incident Diffused ❑ Yes ❑ No Police Notified ❑ Yes ❑ No
Assailant Arrested ❑ Yes ❑ No

13. Disposition of Assailant:
❑ Stayed on Premises ❑ Escorted off Premises ❑ Left on Own ❑ Other

14. Restraints Used: ❑ Yes ❑ No Type:_____

15. Report Completed By:_____ Title:_____
Witnesses:_____
Supervisor Notified:_____ Time:_____

Please put additional comments, according to numbered section, on reverse side of form.

Source: Reprinted with permission of the Metropolitan Chicago Healthcare Council, *Guidelines for Dealing with Violence in Health Care*, Chicago, IL, 1995.

Appendix C
Suggested Readings

Alspach, G. (1993). "Nurses as Victims of Violence." *Critical Care Nurse* 13(5):13–17.

Biles, P.D. (1997). "OSHA's Guidelines for Protecting Health Care Workers from Workplace Violence." *Joint Commission on Accreditation of Healthcare Organizations: Environment of Care/PTSM Series* 3:29–35.

Cal/OSHA. (1998). "Guidelines for Security and Safety of Health Care and Community Service Workers." www.dir.ca.gov/dosh/dosh%5Fpublications/hcworker.html

Carroll, V. and Morin, K.H. (1998). "Workplace Violence Affects One-Third of Nurses." nursingworld.org/tan/98sepoct/violence.htm

Centers for Disease Control and Prevention, National Institute for Occupational Health. (2002). "Occupational Hazards in Hospitals." DHHS (NIOSH) Pub. No. *2002–101*. www.cdc.gov/niosh/2002-101.html

Centers for Disease Control and Prevention, National Institute for Occupational Safety and Health. (1996). "Violence in the Workplace: Risk Factors and Preventive Strategies." *Current Intelligence Bulletin 57*, DHHS (NIOSH) Pub. No. 96-100. www.cdc.gov/niosh/violcont.html

Colling, R.L. (1997). "Controlling Workplace Violence: A Security Management Plan Approach." *Joint Commission on Accreditation of Healthcare Organizations: Environment of Care/PTSM Series 3:37–47.*

Colorado Nurses Association, Task Force on Workplace Violence. (1998). "Survey on Workplace Violence of Nurses in Seven State Nurses Associations." Available from Colorado Nurses Association, Denver, CO. www.nurses-co.org

Davis, S. (1991). "Violence in Psychiatric Inpatients: A Review." *Hospital and Community Psychiatry* 42:585–590.

DiBenedetto, D.V. (1992). "Occupational Hazards of the Healthcare Industry: Protecting Healthcare Workers." *AAOHN Journal* 43(3):131–137.

Dillon, S. (1992). "Social Workers: Targets in a Violent Society." *New York Times*: Al; Al8, November 1, 1992.

Distasio, C.A. (2002) "Protecting Yourself From Violence in the Workplace." *Nursing 2002* 32(6):58–63. www.nursingcenter.com/library/JournalArticle. asp?Article_ID=273445

Elliott, P.P. (1997). "Violence in Health Care: What Nurse Managers Need to Know." *Nursing Management* 28 (12):38–41.

Fazzone, P.A.; Barloon, L.F.; McConnell, S.J.; and Chitty, J.A. (2000). "Personal Safety, Violence and Home Health." *Public Health Nursing* 17(1):43–52.

Flannery, R.B., Jr. (1995). "Violence in the Workplace." New York: Crossroad Press.

Flannery, R.B., Jr.; Hanson, M.A.; and Penk, W.E. (1994). "Risk Factors for Psychiatric Inpatient Assaults on Staff." *Journal of Mental Health Administration* 21:24–31.

Gates, D.M.; Fitzwater, E.; and Meyer, U. (1999). "Violence Against Caregivers in Nursing Homes." *Journal of Gerontological Nursing* 25(4):12–22.

Gilmore–Hall, A. (2001). "Violence in the Workplace: Are You Prepared?" *American Journal of Nursing* 101(7):55–56.

Hansen, B. (1996). "Workplace Violence in the Hospital Psychiatric Setting." *AAOHN Journal* 44(12):575–580.

Hunter, E. (1997). "Violence Prevention in the Home Health Setting." *Home Healthcare Nurse* 15(6):403–409.

Joint Commission on Accreditation of Healthcare Organizations. (2002). "Comprehensive Accreditation Manual for Hospitals." Oakbrook, IL: JCAHO.

Kinkle, S.L. (1993). "Violence in the Emergency Department: How to Stop it Before it Starts." *American Journal of Nursing* 93(7):22–24.

Morgan, L. (1999). "In Harm's Way: Health Care Professionals Face Increasing Abuse in the Workplace." *Nurseweek*, August 2, 1999. www.nurseweek.com/features/99-8/violence.html

Morrison, E., and Herzog, E. (1992). "What Therapeutic and Protective Measures, As Well As Legal Actions, Can Staff Take When They Are Attacked by Patients?" *Journal of Psychosocial Nursing* 30(7):41–44.

Morrison, E.F. (1993). "Toward a Better Understanding of Violence in Psychiatric Settings: Debunking the Myths." *Archives of Psychiatric Nursing* (7)6:328–335.

Nadwairski, J.A. (1992). "Inner-City Safety for Home Care Providers." *Journal of Nursing Administration* 22(9):42–47.

National Security Institute. (1995). "Guidelines for Workplace Violence Prevention Programs for Health Care Workers in Institutional and Community Settings." nsi.org/library/work/violenc1.html

Ore, T. (2002). "Occupational Assault among Community Care Workers." *Journal of Healthcare Management* 18(1):72–89.

Rippon, T.J. (2000). "Aggression and Violence in Health Care Professions." *Journal of Advanced Nursing* 31(2):452–460.

Rusting Publications. (2001). "What Hospital Security Should be Doing Now to Better Prepare for Future Terrorist Activity." *Hospital Security and Safety Management* 22(6):5–10.

Schulte, J.M., et al. (1998). "Violence and Threats of Violence Experienced by Public Health Workers." *Journal of the American Medical Association* 280(5):439–442.

Simonowitz, J.A. (1995). "Violence in Health Care: A Strategic Approach." *Nurse Practitioner Forum* 6(2):120–129.

Simonowitz, J.A.; Rigdon, J.E.; and Mannings, J. (1997). "Workplace Violence: Prevention Efforts by the Occupational Health Nurse." *AAOHN Journal* 45(6):305–316.

Smith-Pittman, M.H. and McKay, Y.D. (1999). "Workplace Violence in Health Care Environments." *Nursing Forum* 34(3):5–13. www.cinahl.com/cgi-bin/jrlgetarticle?nfor3403

Snyder, W., III. (1994). "Hospital Downsizing and Increased Frequency of Assaults on Staff." *Hospital and Community Psychiatry* 45:378–379.

Sygnatur, E.F. and Toscano, G.A. (2000). "Work-Related Homicides: The Facts." *Compensation and Working Conditions* 5(1). www.bls.gov/opub/cwc/2000/spring/art1full.pdf

University of Iowa, Injury Prevention Research Center. (2001). "Workplace Violence: A Report to the Nation." www.public-health.uiowa.edu/IPRC/NATION.PDF

Worthington, K. and Franklin, P. (2001). "Workplace Violence: What to Do if You're Assaulted." *American Journal of Nursing* 101(4):73.

Worthington, K. (2000). "Violence in the Health Care Workplace." *American Journal of Nursing* 100(11):69–70.

Yassi, A., et al. (1998). "Causes of Staff Abuse in Health Care Facilities: Implications for Prevention." *AAOHN Journal* 46(10):484–491.

www.ingramcontent.com/pod-product-compliance
Lightning Source LLC
Chambersburg PA
CBHW051823170526
45167CB00005B/2128